All Week at Sc

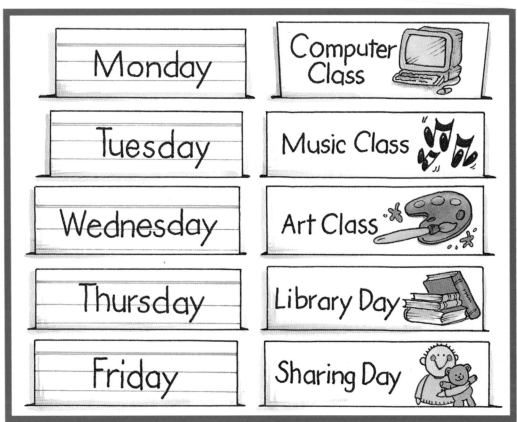

Monday	Computer Class
Tuesday	Music Class
Wednesday	Art Class
Thursday	Library Day
Friday	Sharing Day

We all go to school.
We go on the bus.

We go in cars.
We walk to school.

3

We go on Monday, Tuesday,

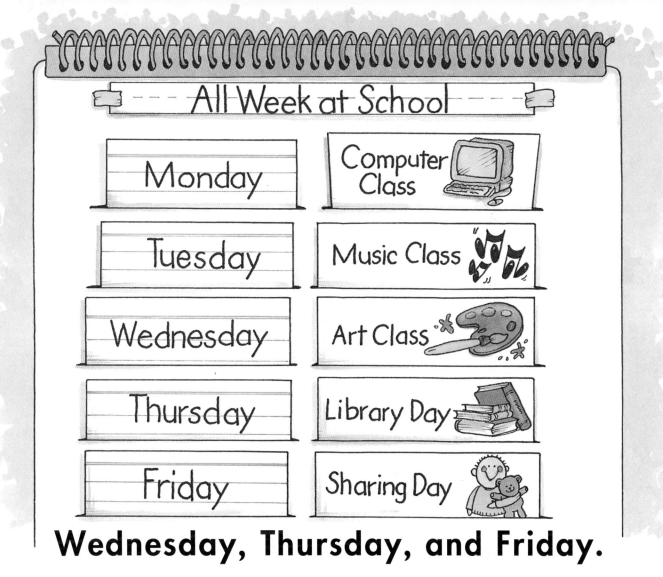

All Week at School

Monday	Computer Class
Tuesday	Music Class
Wednesday	Art Class
Thursday	Library Day
Friday	Sharing Day

Wednesday, Thursday, and Friday.

On Monday, we all have computer class.

We have fun on the computers.

7

On Tuesday, we all have music class.

8

We sing and dance.

On Wednesday, we all have art class.

We paint and draw.

11

We go to the library on Thursday.

We all get books.

On Friday, we all have Sharing Day.

What will I share?

I will share my frog!